GOD OF SEASONS

Michael E. Moynahan, SJ

GOD OF SEASONS

GEORGE ARANHA
2350 Winchester Blvd.
Campbell, Ca 95008
408-378-2464

Michael E. Moynahan, SJ

Published by Resource Publications, Inc.
160 E. Virginia St. #290, San Jose, CA 95112

ISBN 0-89390-019-2
Library of Congress
Catalog Card Number 79-93127

Acknowledgments:
  Cover design and layout: George F. Collopy
  Typography: Virginia Mach

Published by Resource Publications, Inc., 160 E. Virginia St. #290, San Jose, CA 95112

Printed and bound in the United States.

Preface

"In the beginning was the Word...," and that Word of God has lived precariously down through the ages of humankind, heard only where there were prophet lips to speak, hungry hearts to hear. A living Word, made manifest in human speech of all kinds until the very Word came into our midst to speak for Himself. And speak He did. And die He did, gone to live there where all is Life and where He makes ready a home for us who are still on the way. But with Him gone, are we to go Wordless on this bewildering journey of ours?

A living Word. In so many different ways. Alive in us, with our life and we with His. He told us this. A living Word, spoken now not in the accent of Galilee but — and this is a confounding mystery — in accents that are our own, of *our* time and place, of *our* joy and pain, of *our* hope and despair. A living Word, as able now to speak to hungry hearts as once It did on lakeshore and hillside.

For this is what He said: when we speak to one another from the heart, when we listen to one another from the heart, His word lives in us and gives us life. "He who hears you, hears me." It is the very simplicity which eludes us. We do not go Wordless on our journeying. We have one another. If we would but speak what is in our hearts. If we would but listen and hear.

Once again Michael Moynahan speaks from his heart. He speaks of seasons, "natural and liturgical." But what he really speaks is the seasons of the heart. In images that evoke that inner landscape where each of us can think we wander alone, he shows us we are not alone. He calls us to remember — to remember many things, but most of all to remember the ways in which that Beginning Word still lives and gives life, in us and between us.

He is well worth listening to, you who have known the hungers of the heart.

Leo P. Rock, SJ
Loyola Marymount University
Los Angeles, California

Introduction

If one thing characterizes our generation it is forgetfulness. Things move so fast, transportation spans vast distances so quickly, computers produce vast quantities of information at the press of a button. Life moves at such a hectic pace that it is easy to get lost, to get out of tune with ourselves, to get out of touch with nature.

George Harrison once wrote a song entitled "Isn't It A Pity." In the song he powerfully pointed to the tragedy of "forgetting to give back." This is ingratitude. It is precisely those times when we are unmindful that we are ungrateful. Our world is an amnesic world, a forgetful world because we are amnesiacs, forgetters.

What we cry out for today is anamnesis or remembering. We need to remember who we are ourselves, who we are in relation to others, who we are in relationship to God. The seasons, natural and liturgical, are two fundamental ways we can recapture our ability to "remember" and "give thanks."

If we will stop, if we will take them in and be present to them, seasons can help us understand as yet unexplored areas of "who we are" and "what we are about." Too often we ignore or refuse to admit into our lives the very symbols which are passagesways into the depth and mystery of our existence.

Seasons are everpresent. We may refuse them entrance into our consciousness. We may deny them the real power and healing they can have for us. But regardless of our refusals and denials: they have been, they are now, and they will continue to be one of the principle fabrics of our lives.

Seasons have the power to reawaken in us two attributes which we desperately need today: memory and gratitude. I can never genuinely give thanks for what I am unaware of. Memory makes me aware. It reminds me who I am in relation to myself, my neighbor, my God. It situates me temporally and spatially. It brings continuity into my life by pointing out where I have been and the direction in which I am going.

In the beginning God created the world and he gave the earth her seasons. Later, men and women learned a lesson from nature and created liturgical seasons which focused and directed worship. Both do one thing and the same. They call us to stop, to remember and re-experience the giftedness of all of life through her seasonal faces. These faces may be winter/spring/summer/fall or advent/christmas/epiphany/lent/easter/pentecost.

The seasons invite us to enter more fully into life, human existence in all its expressions: clarity and hiddenness, life and death. And by remembering, and by experiencing the gift of our humanity more fully, we may once again rediscover how to give thanks. We do this best by accepting the gift, by enjoying it, by sharing it.

I hope this small book helps me to share that gift with you. I would like to thank in a special way those who by their life and example have helped me experience and remember that God's presence and love is always in season. To my mother, Helen, who never forgets; to my father, Aloysius Pancrasius Valentine

Moynahan, my brother, Tim, and his wife,
Jeannine, whom I remember with deep
affection; and to my brother, Dave, and his
wife, Kay, to my sister, Maureen, and her
husband, Joe, to my sister, Kathy, who all fill
me with great gratitude; in memory and
gratitude to you, I dedicate this book. Your
faith, hope and love have supported and
shaped me in and out of season. By who you
all are, you help me remember and give thanks
daily.

May these prayer-poems help you who read
them to pause and touch again the wondrous
depths of God's presence and love in this
moment, this season he has given us.

Michael E. Moynahan, SJ
Jesuit School of Theology at Berkeley

Contents

Credo

I believe in the goodness of all creation.
I believe in myself and every other unique
    creation called a person.
I believe people were created not to exist
    in isolation but to live, to love, to discover,
    to wonder together in community.
I believe in life and death.
I believe that there is never death without life
    nor life without death.
I believe in wonder, in surprise, in spontaneity
    and creativity and everything childlike.
I believe that the childlike is the Godlike.
Only God and the child can watch with
incomparable
    joy and awe at the absurdity and splendor of
the
    creation of their hands and love it because it
is theirs.
I believe that unless we are children
    we will miss God or so distort him
    that what we see and meet will bear little
resemblance
to the reality which is his person.
So I believe in letting the child in each of us
grow.

I believe in the big and extraordinary
    as being just that: big and extraordinary.
I believe in the common, ordinary, small and
    insignificant because they are just that.
In exaggerating the value of the first and
underestimating
    the value and significance of the second,
I believe we distort life and let our real
encounters
    with God in the human pass us by.
I believe in jumping into life and engaging in
life.
I pity the spectator.

I want to be immersed in life and not view it
    at a distance as a disinterested observer.
I believe in hope, in faith, in love,
    in any and everything from whose seeds
spring life.
I do not believe in fear or anything which only
destroys
or breaks down or makes life impossible or
meaningless.
I believe in faith because the faith others
placed in me
    has enabled me to grow and believe in
others.
I believe in hope because it is the fertilizer of
life.
Without it there is no growth, no end of day,
    no sunrise to greet each day.
I believe in love because the love of others
has awakened love in me and me to love.

I believe faith, hope and love are perfectly
summed up
    in Jesus Christ.
God so loved the world, believed so much in
the goodness
    of all he had created, that he wanted to ratify
and reaffirm
    creation's goodness and give men and
women a reminder
    for all time.
And so, prompted by faith and compelled by
love, God's son
became one of us, a human being, Jesus Christ,
and thus
    became our hope.
Jesus came to make God accessible, knowable,
    so that we might see, hear and touch him.
He told us once and for all what his Father
desires:
    that we love one another.

He explained the mystery of love:
   that in loving that other person —
   our wife, our husband, our child,
a stranger or friend —
God is touched and his love becomes real
again.

All of this I believe.

Satisfying Somethings

O God,
you speak so quietly,
your word and call
compete with constant noise:
the thousand sounds
that blare and drone
at twenty-thousand decibels.

Undiluted volume groans
cacaphonic melodies
that strangle, smother,
completely drown
your gentle, little
whisperings.

My ears are deaf
to softer tones.
My hearing has abandoned me.
My life has fallen flat
into a stultifying
monotone.

This pilgrim's numb
from hunger
for a word
that will not only fill
but satisfy
the feelings
of a battered heart!

Come quickly,
gentle Lord,
and whisper now
into this empty,
aching heart,
your sweet
and satisfying
somethings.

God Of Seasons

O God of seasons,
Lord of Spring,
whose face we see
in everything that lives
and moves or makes up life,
we thank you
for these simple gifts.

For freedom found
in open skies
and secrets wrapped
in ocean depths,
for life that bursts
from caves of death,
for signs of hope
that circle us
and tempt us to
a faith that stands
against so many shouted doubts,
for all of this
we give you thanks.

Our eyes confront
the mystery
that wonder-fills us
everyday:
the timid-dazed excitement
of unsteady bird's first flight,
leave-taking of the world it knew,
for unknown things that lie ahead.
Found only in the flying —
inevitable dying
to what once was
so hidden hoped-for things
can blossom into life
from bubbled possibility.

Renew us,
God of paradox,
so we can enter
into life.
Help us let go
of everything:
the fought for life
that we would hoard,
the fears that will
not let us die
or fly into eternity.
Come now and rinse
our ashened mouths
so we can say
that dirty word
we cannot hear.
Let its ever present power
strengthen our
unfaithful hearts.
Come work your magic
in our lives,
draw life from death
and exorcise us of
our dread-full reasoning.
Do now, your wonder
full of resurrection
here, among us.

Hidden God

Lord of winter,
God of cold,
whose presence
we are often told
is unobtrusive,
almost imperceptible,
let us catch
a passing glance
of things to come.
Enhance our sometimes
anxious wait:
the painful passage
of fear-filled days,
worry-weakened
winter dreams,
chilled delays.
Come help us see
what frozen eyes
are blinded to:
the life that slowly
comes to be
below the surface
sight of things
(silent night,
quiet life that's
cloaked in snow).

O hidden God,
you quite confound us
with your presence
underground.
Frost-bitten faith
is wearing thin,
weak from fasting,
looking hard
for lasting confirmation
of longed for
comings to be.

Lightsome God,
send us sun:
your spirit's
warming breath.
Unfreeze us,
ease our doubt,
free our frozen faith
and icy dreams.
Teach us once again
your mystery sent in season:
a rousing encore
of life from death.
Come swiftly,
quickening Lord.
Let winter thaw
and gift our hearts
with spring.

God Who Comes

O God,
whose advent we await,
come quickly now
and gift us with your presence.

We seem to spend
countless hours waiting,
watching,
straining hard to catch
a first-class glimpse
of him whom we have never,
can never seem to recognize.
Waiting for Godot?
Waiting for heaven's sake?
No! For our sake.
Waiting for —
God only knows
what we are waiting for.
He knows.
God knows.
He must know!
Please, God, know
we are waiting for you.

And how shall we know you,
or what shall we call you,
when you do come,
illusive, fleeting,
seeding inspiration
and tantalizing phantom
of our make-believe world?

You are light
for our weary eyes.
You are counsel
that fills us wonder-full again.
You are the price of peace:
a prince who steps down
from your throne
to hear our cries,
to feel our pain,
to see the desperate need
of all of us
to be renewed
and slowly learn the way
back to belief
and hope and love.
You are the faces, races,
the hopes and hurts,
the healing, hearts and hands
that surround, confuse,
confound us.
You are the Christ,
the Son of God,
buried, hidden,
locked forever in the timeless
longings of our hearts.

Then quickly come,
approaching God!
Make us.
Recreate us.
Help us believe again
in you, ourselves,
and this our world.

Incarnation

O God,
who sees our every need,
when we had wandered
from your love,
You bent down low
and touched the earth.
You kissed us in our ugliness.
Your oh so gently whispered Word
crept quietly into our hearts.

Softly did he climb down
deep into our wound —
the womb of possibility
where calluses had covered over
pain-filled fears,
tears, years of frustration
eating what never satisfied,
drinking deeply a thousand things
that could not quench our thirst.

And then, one day,
You, goodly God,
looked again on what you made.
And seeing people stumbling blind,
hopelessly so deaf and dumb,
living a tortured kind of death,
your faithful heart went out to us.
It almost broke
watching all you loved despair.

And somewhere, in an unknown place,
deep within you ached and groaned,
waters flooded Father's eyes
overflowing, enduring promised love.
Something fell from your kind sight
that broke the hush of night's expectancy
and drenched our parched shattered hopes,
our tattered dreams
and war torn world.

Your Word was heard
in noiseless splashing.
On that less or more than silent night
he pitched his tent
and walked with us
to heal our hurting earth.
We thank you, Lord, for Jesus' birth:
that saving drop
of godly goodness.

Christmas Lullaby

Little boy,
little boy,
are those tears
in your eyes?
Can you see
all we need?
Can you taste
our poverty?
Can you teach me
to care for someone else?
I am imprisoned
in thoughts of myself.

Little boy,
Little boy,
can you hear
people cry?
Can you heal
aching hearts?
Can you bring
peace on earth?
How can you heal
the hurts of countless years?
Can a baby free us
from all of our fears?

Little boy,
little boy,
you are clothed
in mystery.
Can our hope
be disguised
in one so young,
in one so wise?

Fill us full
of all that satisfies.
Teach us how to live
and never fear to die.

Little boy,
little boy,
can you sleep?
Can you dream?
We have played
mournful tunes.
We have waited
far too long.
Wake and hear
our desperate pleading prayer.
Through your gentle coming
teach us how to care.

Anna's Song

Lord of my life
I wait for you
in the morning,
in the evening,
just for you.

As a child
when I grew up
I learned to look ahead
with expectation.
So with all
your little ones
I waited
for your coming.

Lord of my days
I long for you
in the morning,
in the evening,
just for you.

Eighty years
you came to me
disguised in wounded hearts
and desperate faces.
You taught me
how to find you
in the needs
of all around me.

My heart's desire
you come to me
in the morning,
in the evening,
everywhere.

I thank you for
the thousand deaths
I had to die in order
to be born again.
I thank you
for you gift me
with salvation
every day.

Lord of my life
I wait for you
in the morning,
in the evening,
just for you.
My heart's desire
you come to me.
You're my morning,
you're my evening,
you're my life.

Epiphany

O God,
 who's hidden deep within
the timeless yearnings
of our hearts,
you trigger something
in us all
that makes us restless,
anxious for discovery
of what will satisfy
new felt wanderlust.

Like kings before
who searched the sky
and recklessly pursued a dream
they hoped was more than make-believe,
we, too, leave all we know
and travel into unknown lands
driven madly day and night
by what our hapless startling hope
can only guess at.

Our journey's filled
with constant doubt
and ever-present fear.
How will we know
when we have found
travel's impulse,
this craving we call
our heart's desire?

In our search
we leave no stone unturned.
We struggle frantically
to find our happiness
perhaps in this town.

Or when we meet
with failure here
our sight adjusts instinctively
to over the horizon there
where we will next settle
for a resting place.

Then one day,
as every pilgrimage
must run its course,
when hope is drained
and body broke,
we'll find ourselves in Bethlehem
weary, wounded, travelled out.
And so we'll stumble,
as if by accident,
into epiphany.

How could three travellers
with dust-filled eyes
see such good
in one so young?
Had we come all that way for this?
And once again we bruise our heads
bumping into mystery.
The child found there
will touch and free
the child in us.

And we will feel
somewhat renewed
for having found in him
what lies deepest
in every pilgrim's heart.

O God, who's found in journey's end,
bless all our goings,
fill all our comings,
help us all be freed
and found by you.

God Who Wanders Into View

O God, who wanders into view,
you gift us with wisdom's guide
who sees and points you out to us
as you pass by.
Our heads and hearts are everywhere
scattered over all the earth
looking hard for answers that will
quiet questions from within;
scouring earth and sea and sky
for just one Word that will satisfy.

And so somehow mysteriously
we follow you: at first attracted,
then compelled, for urgency
has found our feet.
So we hurry after you
drawn on as if magnetized.
Then you stop and turn.
We almost stumble over you
but catching caution soon enough
we freeze fast in our steps.

We nervously avoid your eyes
and feel hearts pulsing, pounding,
lodged and trapped
in trembling throats.
You do not quickly speak to us.
Instead, you ease the awkwardness
with silence, a penetrating glance.
You looked so hard at us
we felt embarrassment,
confused by what you may
or may not see.

And finally a sound comes forth,
your words with deadly accuracy
find their way to where we live.
"What do you want?"
What do we want?
Have you got three good years to spend
listening to how our story goes:
our little faith, our squandered hopes,
the hundred thousand things we've felt
we've needed, sought,
and fought like hell for?
And much, much, more!

Then suddenly our words fall short.
Your question, so simply put
breaks through the garbage
of our twisted feelings
and agonizing minds.
"What do you want?"
Somehow what was certainty is gone,
replaced by one clear longing —
to be with you.
For you, in a brief moment's passing
have captured a young fisherman's heart.

Much more than simple curiosity aroused —
though some of that.
No, we were captured by his face
a gentle, strong, warm presence.
He took us by surprise
with eyes whose depth we could not fathom.
In them lay the played out
hopes and fears, laughter, tears
of generations past and still to come.

"Where do you dwell?"
Oh tell us quickly, now!
Let us quench this monstrous thirst.
You will let us, but not all at once.
You give no facile remedies.
Invitation's your reply.
"Come and see."

That simple answer: "Come and see"
filled with endless possibility:
a pilgrim's path composed
if at times unevenly
of struggles, trials — the agony;
and then those moments of reward,
the rest that comes to weary feet,
the joy that's found in discovery.

And so, led on by God knows what,
we follow you.
We drag along our doubts and fears,
our fragile, often dashed hopes,
in many broken pieces.
We also bring with us desire:
a fire you first breathed into us
when you turned and looked with love
on two timid, frightened followers.

O God who calls us,
come and spend some time with us.
Pass an evening at our fires
and touch in us our deepest wants.

Wedding Prayer

God of our humanity,
we thank you for becoming
flesh again
in Brian and Rita's
love.

Thank you
for creating us
and calling us
to live with others.

And though solitude and loneliness,
silence and distance
are important parts
of every human life,
thank you for companionship,
for shared love,
for marriage,
for family and community.

You touch us, Lord,
when we touch one another.
You speak to us,
when we speak to each other.
You heal us, kiss us, make us new
when we heal, kiss and renew
all those who live around us.
You love us, Lord,
and your love is made real again,
when we love one another.

Lord,
may Brian and Rita
learn to be faithful
to each other
just as you are faithful
to all of us.

May they offer each other
friendship
when they are lonely.
May they comfort each other
in their sorrow
and share each other's happiness.
May their pain be real
and all their joys intense.
May nothing human
ever pass them by.

May they be made rich
by the love and support
of good friends.
May they enrich others
by prodigally giving
of their love and friendship.

Help them, Lord,
be silent at times.
Teach them to listen to each other
and in this way hear you.
Let their words and eyes and hands
express the strength and depth
of all that their hearts feel.

May they know a parent's joy
and share with you in creation.
Teach them to bless
their own children, family and friends
with the faith, the hope and love
that have brought them together
today.

And finally, Lord,
may they always be one:
one in adversity
one in their happiness;
one when it's easy
and one when it's hard;
one in mind and body and heart.
Together may they grow
in their heart's desire
to be one in their love
forever.

Amen.

Palm Sunday

Knowledge of finality.
Concluding quickly
what had been,
some short time ago,
begun.

Facing now
those last few days
with what?
A burst of celebration.
A crowd of half-crazed
Roman-riddled Jews
shouting
for all they're worth:
"Blessings on —
whoever comes to save us!"

Just how does one
bow out gracefully?
Useless to explain again
what three years'
word and work
have constantly
moved towards.
Thought by many
possessed, insane;
anticipating unknown pain;
moving with such
stern resolve
to yet another disappointment
for my people ——
the last great disaster:
that paschal mystery thing.

Filled with memories
that flood an aching heart
and tired mind.
Every healing, teaching,
contradictory feeling,
tireless reaching out
to simple, hungry people —
all solitary stones.

Pieced together, though,
they paved the way
to this:
confusion's reign,
the frightening recurrence
of sorrow's familiar face,
the loss of those
whose love he knew,
shattered dreams
reluctantly forgotten,
wasted possibilities,
the endless taunt
of haunting questions,
and last, but not least,
that ultimate defeat —
Death —
and whatever lies
beyond death's door:
(That hoped for place
we only dare whisper of
in soft, hushed tones.
A place where all old bones
are catastrophically reborn.)
a New Jerusalem.

Holy Thursday

Friends meeting
one final time
in life as he knew it.
The thought of things
presently to come
weighing heavily
on his heart.

And others seeing
no more nor less
than what wine-dulled sense
can glean from appearances:
something they had done
with predicted regularity
long before this
momentous time arrived.
Gathered with friends,
celebrating that
passing-over event.

My how time flys
when one is having
a good time!
Minutes ticking past.
Too fast!
Too little time left!

Three years walking,
talking, teaching,
reaching out in hope
and calling forth
the good in each:
healing for
the seasoned cynic
in us all.

So it now
comes down to this:
leave-taking.
What to say?
What to do?
So much to say.
So much to do.
All poured into this
last parting gesture:
a sign,
a prayer.
Relying on
memory's gift
and what a transformed meal
can possibly recall
celebrated
miles and years
from here and now
with people gathered
in his name.

Good Friday

Sprung from disaster
the result of much strife.
Confounding all reason
death produces life.

Perennial confusion
blinds weary eyes
as from burnt ashes
a Phoenix will rise.

A problem perplexing,
a mystery profound:
dead seed's new borning —
life underground.

Irony unparalleled,
a paradox encored:
in sharing bread and wine —
Christ proclaimed Lord!

Easter Sunday

Wheat grains crushed
provide our food.

grape full bunches pressed
become our table drink.

because they do not cling
to what they were,

a wonderful new happening:
our paschal meal.

we who are hungry —
fed;

we who are thirsty —
satisfied;

we who were empty —
filled;

we who were dead —
alive again!

Proudly rising:
new life from old ashes.

death never again the end
only a stop on the journey.

But new things also die
to come again in unimagined ways.

bread broken becomes a meal —
signs us a community.

wine passed around and shared
becomes our cup of blessing.

and when we eat
and when we drink
we remember.

our eyes are opened a little more
and we know:

this is the bread of life,
this is the cup of our salvation.

so we eat,
we drink,
we die,
but most importantly
we rise.

Alleluia!
Come Lord Jesus!

again,
and again,
and again.

Death

Good God,
why all these tears?
You see our wrinkled brows
and wounded hearts.
Why come so unexpectedly?
Why take us by surprise?
You call us now to dance and play
when we are frozen fast
in our anxiety.
Why gift us with
this painful presence?
Are you hiding there —
somewhere to be found —
in paralyzing grief?

Memory of times gone by
when you were near.
You walked and talked
and wandered freely
in our company.
So real, so reassuring
that our touch and taste,
our eyes and ears
all shouted loud
your goodness was not make-believe.

Memories of time:
good times,
any time but this time.
Death is no time.
It knows nothing.
It waits for nothing.
If you had only prepared us,
warned us of this new thing:
Nothing!

Fragile memories
that falter, fade,
paled by the reality
of nuisance death.
Nonsense?
Perhaps.

We ache for answers
never there.
We rummage frantically
through what were
faith-filled cupboards —
now deserted, bare.
Not just life
but one-time hopes
seem lost —
buried under quarts
of tear-filled fears.

Draw near to us,
you Lord of life.
Come help us now
believe again.
Awaken hope
in all whose memory has dimmed.
Give us the healing peace
of your consoler.
Unblind, unbind us
so we see you standing with us
in our sorrows.
Help us cling to nothing:
not life, not death,
not even wholesome grief.
Let your faithfulness and care
renew once more
our shaken trust in you.

A Pilgrim's Prayer

Father, I have come to experience your love
  in many ways
As life's Pilgrim.
I thank you for the spirit you breathed
  into me — a wandering spirit —
For eyes that guide me, feet that plod the
  paths,
occassional sign posts when I have lost the way.
But most of all I thank you for your love
Which has given my journey meaning and
  direction.
You have blessed me with your divine
  restlessness,
Prodded me from my complacency, urged me
  down roads
I would not feel strong enough to travel,
Supported me with fellow-travelers
Who bolstered me when I despaired,
  refreshed and renewed me
When I thought my last step was just that.
How am I to show my thanks for life and
  breath,
For eyes and limbs, for companionship
On an otherwise lonely journey?
Why I, your Pilgrim, in the company of your
  vagabonds
Whom you have joined me to,
  accept the gifts you have given me
And promise to use them all as I struggle to
  grapple
With the journey out and the journey in,
The mystery of your presence in me,
  in us, in my world, in our world.
Help me to avail myself of the freedom you
  bring.

Never let me forget I am a Pilgrim on the way
   home.
Teach me to seek you, meet you,
   and know you as I travel the way.
Especially I pray that you give me faithful
   companions
Who will let me rest — but never stop,
Who will challenge me in my comfortableness,
Strengthen me in my weakness,
Support me in the sufferings all journeys
   involve
And share with me the joy of traveling,
Seeking and finding our way home together.
This I ask through Christ,
Your Son and my brother,
The Pilgrim and the way,
Now and forever.

Amen.

Suscipe

We offer you, Lord,
a poor man's gift.
We offer you a poor man's life.
We're poor and hungry;
we're naked and weak;
we break easily, Lord,
so handle us gently.

The goods that we offer
are gifts from you:
our lives with all their freedom,
our distracted minds,
our often weak wills,
and failing memories.
These are a poor man's gift to you.

And since they came from you, Lord,
please see your way clear to accepting them.
We've had our problems using them well,
but we know your love can transform them
into a gift pleasing to you.

And as for us, Lord,
hear your servant's simple prayer:
When we are weak, be our strength;
when we doubt, be our faith;
when we're discouraged, be our hope;
and when we're lost,
come and find us.
When we're hungry, be our food;
when we're thirsty, be our drink;
when we're in darkness, be our light;
and when we're sad,
be our comfort and joy.

Let us feel your touch
in all we say and do.
Let us grow and blossom
in your love.
Grant us this, Lord,
and there's nothing more we want
until we see you face to face.
Take all we have and all we are;
give us your love and your grace,
with these we are full,
yes, we're full.

The Word That Satisfies

O God whose word
is food and drink
to pain-full bellies,
ease our hunger.
Quench a pilgrim's
parched-throat thirst.

Look with pity
on a people
who once upon a time ago
flourished;
imaged glory of our maker;
now, over-indulged
and undernourished.
Greed and gluttony
have left their marks.
We've gorged ourselves
on countless feedings
and walked away unsatisfied,
starved for one authentic piece
of understanding,
or what could transubstantiate
the simplest things
into a meal:
an ounce of true companionship.

We've tasted fruit
from a thousand trees:
knowledge, wealth, morality.
None have freed us.
Our lives are spent
in restlessness:
nomadic searching
for some tiny inn
or ounce of satisfaction,

that illusive Shangri-la
where we can settle down
and never feel again
the bite of hunger,
pinch of thirst.

O God whose table's
set in stark simplicity,
your word is bread
for hungry souls.
It satisfies the longings
of all empty-aching hearts.
Draw us, tattered, tainted,
(anything but sainted) pilgrims
around your table, now.
Be drink for those
who thirst for peace.
Help us live
with all our ambiguity,
the paradoxes
of daily life:
faith in the face
of shouted doubts,
hope that looks for
life from death,
love that seeks
not self but others.

Forgiving God?

Lord,
help me find it in my heart
to forgive you
for making me the way I am.
Blasphemy? Perhaps.
Honesty? For lack of a better word, yes.
In this one repeated blinding
moment of clarity
I honestly need to forgive you, Lord.
I know I am the work of your hands.
I have experienced your gentle touch
in summer breezes
and the warmth of winter fires.
I meet your love in many ways.
In the emptiness of silence
and plentitude of sound;
In light-some revelations
of colorful, moving, living things;
In dead dark night
and still-filled noises;
In thoughts that soar
and feelings that pound;
In good times, bad times, high and lows,
sleeping, waking, seasonally, annually,
every way, everywhere,
each second past,
life-filled full
momentous day,
I am surrounded by your love.

Is it madness, then,
or simply blindness
that keeps me so shortsighted?
Perhaps a bit of both impairs my vision
and will not let the good outside
be seen within.

What reason, traitor? Treason!
I cannot see.
I do not know.
So many things I cannot see.
So many things I do not know.

I have been told you made me
like yourself.
Why then do we two
think so differently?
You made me what I am, Lord.
There is so much I cannot understand,
so much I cannot thank you for.
You who first shared love with me
and showed me how to live;
You whose heart is poured out in creation
and found in forgiveness;
Teach me to forgive your constant
kindnesses to me.

Forgive Me, Lord

For the times I run and hide, Lord,
for the times I deal in death
with frozen words
and frosted smiles,
left over touches
and warmed up stares,
forgive me.

For all the ways that I am blind:
For all the times I close my eyes,
the many wounded I walk by,
the hungry starving for a word,
and those who thirst
for an ounce of care,
for bodies bared and naked souls
spirits who need compassion's clothes,
for prisoners who need someone's touch
for sure release from phantom fears,
for the lonely who seek companionship,
the homeless who need community,
For all who come across my path
with outstretched hands
and open hearts,
for all of those I turn away
to meet you, Lord,
another time,
another place......
Forgive me, Lord,
for I'm so blind.

For all the ways that I am deaf
to other people's needs and cries:
for clinging to security,
for tackling only the conquerable,
for doing things the easy way,
for playing my deceitful games,
for strength that distances me from them,
forgive me, Lord.

For all the times I think I'm God,
or act in ways that say as much,
for being ashamed of all I am
and disowning my humanity,
for all the ways I make it hard
for you, O Lord, to become flesh,
forgive me.
Put my weary wayward feet
once more upon the path to you.

Your fidelity and love bewilder me.
You always find me when I'm lost,
You comfort me when I am sad,
You tend to me when I am hurt.
And now I ask your healing love
for all the times and ways I fail.
And even now I thank you, Lord,
for I know you hear my prayers.

Veils We Hide Behind

Attend to us,
forgiving God!

You see the many veils
we hide behind:
the ways we numb ourselves
with drugs and booze,
with glaring sights
and pounding sounds,
that dull our senses
and blind us to reality.
You read our hearts
and know the hurt we work
on one another.

You made us like yourself
and showed us how to walk in light.
You taught us through your son
how to reveal ourselves
for who we really are:
children of a loving Lord.

But somehow we discovered caves
and thought they cost much less.
We uttered unconvincing words —
they were more comfortable.
And so, we find them
everyday, every way
playing on this deadly game
of hide and seek.

Darkness covers best
our broken dreams
and hopes of what could be.
We forgot how fragile
was our heart's desire.
And so the splintered pieces
of squandered possibilities
lay lifeless on the floor
of gone-by days.

Come seek us out
and find us,
loving God!
Come work your reconciling wonder
in our midst again.
Draw us out of darkness
into light.
Instill in us
the trust and care
and deep desire for oneness
that make of fear-filled hiders,
images of you.

Remember And Give Thanks

Oh, the power of meals in our life!
Family and friends eating, being fed
with food and drink and presence.
Have you ever noticed how meals can tap
that vast unlistened to and disregarded
treasure house of memories?
REMEMBER AND GIVE THANKS.

Meals always begin with grace.
They sometimes end with grace.
And all that passes in between
can challenge
the very meaning of grace.
REMEMBER AND GIVE THANKS.

Time to count our blessings!
But where does one begin?
How does one begin?
The grocery list of gifts received
reaches back before this time, this place,
and stretches far beyond
the whispered, hoped-for dreams
of distant days to come.
REMEMBER AND GIVE THANKS.

Where does one begin?
Here. Today. And let today
call up those yesterdays
and point us all towards
only guessed at visions
of tomorrow.
Where does one begin?
REMEMBER AND GIVE THANKS.

How does one begin?
Here we simply have no rules.
Some proceed quite logically.
Others move creatively.
Some proceed as children do
simply with spontaneity.
Others do not move so fast
and demonstrate complexity.
Some proceed with clarity
others only haltingly.
How does one begin?
REMEMBER AND GIVE THANKS.

Continuity.
It is now.
It was yesterday.
It will be tomorrow.
What matter if it be
rain-filled or sun-drenched?
Brightness, darkness,
sorrow, joy: feelings
shout you are alive.
Find the gift in everything.
REMEMBER AND GIVE THANKS.

What better way than gathering now,
together breaking all we have:
the bread of our lives —
memory of days gone by
and hoped-for possibilities;
and the wine that makes us glad —
reminding us
that gifts should be enjoyed.
Joined in gift and memory
we shout aloud our heartfelt thanks
by eating, drinking,
sharing yet another gift.
REMEMBER AND GIVE THANKS,

Michael Moynahan, SJ is a campus minister at Santa Clara University. A native of Phoenix, Arizona, he entered the Society of Jesus in 1962. Ordained in 1973, Father Moynahan was assistant Director of Novices for the California Province from 1973-1976, and taught liturgy and drama for several years at the Jesuit School of Theology in Berkeley, California. He is founder of the Berkeley Liturgical Drama Guild, a member of the editorial Board of *Modern Liturgy* magazine, and author of three books: *God of Untold Tales, How the Word Became Flesh,* and *Once Upon a Parable.* All are available from Resource Publications, Inc., 160 E. Virginia St. #290, San Jose, CA 95112.